Copyright © 2024 by Pippa Bird

All rights reserved. No part of this book may be reproduced or transmitted in any form or by any means, electronic or mechanical, including photocopying, recording, or by any information storage and retrieval system, without permission in writing from the publisher.

ISBN: 9781763733992

First Edition

The Loud Crack

One morning, Kiya was munching on eucalyptus leaves when she heard a soft whimpering sound at the base of her tree.

She looked down to see a rather odd looking rock.

Kiya climbed halfway down her tree to investigate.

'I know that rock', she thought to herself, 'only…it's not a rock..'

"Hello, are you in there?" Kiya asked, climbing down from her tree.

"Go away, monster!" Snapped the odd looking rock. Kiya took a step back.

"Monster? I'm not a monster," replied Kiya. "I'm a koala."

"A koala?" Started the tortoise, emerging from its shell.

"Were you the one that made that loud, scary noise just a moment ago?" asked the tortoise, worried.

"Scary noise? I didn't hear a scary noise. What did it sound like?" Kiya asked.

"It sounded something like k-ch-kkchh. Like a big crack."

"And then there was a thud."

"It sounded like it came from up there. I thought it was coming down to get me," said the tortoise.

Kiya looked toward the tree tops in wonder.

Kiya gently reached out to comfort the trembling tortoise.

"It's okay to feel scared. Let's find a quiet spot and sit together until you feel safe."

They found a cosy patch of grass in a clearing of trees. Kiya sat beside the tortoise and offered her hand for comfort once again.

"I'm Kiya," said the koala.

"My name is Tallulah. My friends call me Talkative, but I don't feel like talking very much right now," spoke the tortoise.

"Tallulah, it's okay not to feel ourselves when we don't feel safe. Being scared is normal. Would you like to take a few deep breaths with me? It might help you calm down."

"Sure, Kiya. If you think that will help."

The new friends closed their eyes and took three deep breaths together.
By doing this, Kiya helped Tallulah calm her trembling body so she could think clearly.

Kiya then began humming a soothing tune. Tallulah soon felt her fear melt away.

"Wow, Kiya. I can feel my body calming…"
Tallulah said with a warm smile.

"That's wonderful, Tallulah. How do you feel about finding that noise you heard?" said Kiya.

Tallulah nodded, feeling a little anxious now.

"It's okay, my friend," started Kiya, "These trees are my home; I know every branch, twig and leaf. And I think I know what sound you heard."

"Are you sure?" asked Tallulah.

"I'm certain, my reptilian friend. And there's one way to find out."

Tallulah trusted Kiya's confidence and followed behind.

Kiya headed straight for her tree.

Kiya had almost reached the top by the time Tallulah had arrived.

The tortoise waited patiently.

Kiya looked around the tree tops in search of where the loud noise came from.

"I FOUND IT," she called out to her friend.

"IT IS RIGHT OVER THERE!"

Kiya started climbing down her tree when she noticed Tallulah had hid inside her shell once more.

Kiya gently reached out to comfort the trembling tortoise again.

"Oh, Tallulah. I found where the terrifying sound came from, and it's really nothing to fear."

"Really, Kiya?"

Kiya smiled and nodded gently.

The koala pointed up toward the tree tops.

"The sound you heard was a loud crack from a tree branch breaking. And the loud thud? Well, it fell to the ground. They do that sometimes. It is perfectly normal"

"Come, I'll show you."

The bush friends found the source of the loud noise. Just as Kiya had said, a tree branch had broken and fallen to the ground.

"Oh, I see," said the tortoise, "It's just a tree branch."

"If you hear that loud noise again, just know that it's a branch or stick, falling from the trees. It happens often. It is normal, and not scary at all," said Kiya.

"Thank you, Kiya. I feel so much better now. Thank you for helping me calm down. You are such an important friend."

"That's okay, Tallulah. Just remember, whenever you feel scared, take a few deep breaths. In and out. In and out."

Kiya showed Tallulah how to practice breathing. They both smiled, enjoying each other's company in the moment of calm.

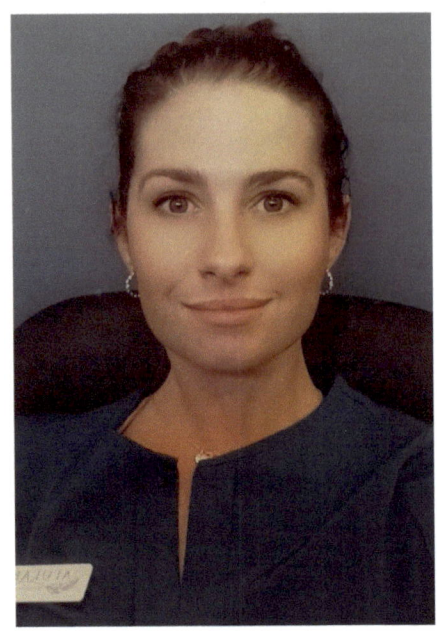

About the Author

Pippa Bird is a Mental Health Therapist in Private Practice in regional NSW. Pippa holds a Bachelor in Psychology, a Diploma in Counselling, and is currently undertaking a Postgraduate Degree in the field.

Pippa also holds a Diploma in Graphic Design, with a primary focus on illustration.

Calm Kangaroo

CALM KANGAROO is a backronym title for a children's mental well-being program. An initiative designed to educate children about mental health and foster a learning journey of emotional intelligence, resilience and cultivate an open mind through the power of reading well-being books, leading to the most important discussions and ideas.

The CALM KANGAROO program focuses on **C**urating, **A**dvocating and **L**eading **M**indfulness and its mission to **K**indle **A**wareness, **N**urture **G**rowth, **A**mplify **R**esilience, and **O**rchestrate **O**pen-minds.

Calm Kangaroo is an Alula Blu Initiative

www.ingramcontent.com/pod-product-compliance
Lightning Source LLC
Chambersburg PA
CBHW041543040426
42446CB00003B/221